MEDICAL IMAGES CLASSIFICATION USING DEEP LEARNING

MEFTAHI Z.HANANE

List of abbreviations

AI	Artificial Intelligence
ANN	Artificial Neural Network
BNN	Biological Neural Network
CAD	Computer-Aided Detection and Diagnosis
CADe	Computer-Aided Detection
CADx	Computer-Aided Diagnosis
CNN	Convolutional Neural Network
DDSM	Digital Database For Screening Mammography
FDA	Food and Drug Administration
IDC	Invasive Ductal Carcinoma
KNN	K-nearest Neighbors
ML	Machine Learning
ONEIROS	Open-ended Neuro-Electronic Intelligent Robot Operating System
ReLU	Rectified Linear Unit
ResNet	Residual Neural Network
RNN	Recurrent Neural Network
SVM	Support Vector Machines
VGG	Visual Geometry Group

Summary

List of figures

List of tables

General introduction

Medical imaging is without a doubt one of the areas of medicine that has progressed the most in the previous two decades. It is utilized for illness prevention, identification of a specific spectrum of diseases, and reliable tracking of illness progression.

Breast cancer has become a public health issue in recent decades. It is one among the world's top causes of mortality among women. Breast cancer patients arrive in hospitals at a tardy stage, when even the most cutting-edge therapies are futile. As a result, cancer screening and early detection remain critical in the fight against this illness.

The ultimate radiographic test for detecting abnormalities in women's breasts is mammography. It collects pictures that aid in the detection of malignant cells using low doses of X-rays.

Medical practitioners are dealing with more and more numerous, complicated, and diverse data: exams have become more varied, and data complexity has increased. Exploiting data without the aid of a processing system is getting difficult.

The aim of this book is to introduce readers to Deep Learning techniques and help them develop models and algorithms in order to assist in the analysis and interpretation of mammograms.

If determining the specific causes of breast cancer remains challenging, it may be possible to build a Computer-Aided Diagnosis (CAD) to assist radiologists in recognizing it early and so making treatment more successful.

Besides the introduction and the conclusion, this book is structured in four chapters.

In the 1st chapter, I will present the CAD technology, detail its structure and enumerate its field of applications.

In the 2nd chapter, I will introduce the most popular images categorization approaches "Clustering and Classification", give a brief description of Machine learning, and its known techniques, recall classification in supervised learning, and present some of its algorithms.

In the 3rd chapter, I will define Deep Learning, Artificial Neural Networks, the basics of CNNs, how they are used in conjunction, and how features are not hand engineered but learned.

In the 4th chapter, we will develop a Deep Learning model from scratch and exploit one of the pre-trained models used in production with different fine-tuning methods for mammograms classification.

Chapter 1: Computer-Aided Detection and Diagnosis in medical imaging

Introduction

CAD is a computer-based technology that incorporates components of artificial intelligence and computer vision with radiological and pathology image processing. It is composed of two subsystems, the first subsystem is computer-aided detection (CADe) and the second subsystem is computer-aided diagnosis (CADx) grouped under the acronym CAD, which can be used to assist medical professionals in providing accurate diagnosis to patients, it can serve radiologists as a second opinion for image interpretation, hence its importance in the medical field.

For a long time, it has been perceived that even the best human observers make mistakes in the interpretation of images. Errors may be attributed to many causes including flawed visual perception or erroneous analysis. Thus, recognition software might be needed, this is where Computer-aided detection (CADe) comes into action. It detects and emphasize questionable elements on the image to radiologists, so as to lessen false negative readings. This is different from the concept of computer aided diagnosis (CADx), which designate a software that analyses a radiographic finding to estimate the tendency that the feature represents a specific disease (e.g. benign versus malignant).

This chapter introduces CAD technology, presents a brief history of CAD and discusses its application areas.

I.   A brief history of CAD

In recent years, with the advancement of computer technology, CAD has achieved fast development in medical fields in the developed countries, especially in the field involving medical imaging. Practice has shown that CAD has played a very active role in improving the accuracy of diagnosis, decreasing missed diagnosis, and improving work efficiency [1].

The CAD appliance in medicine can be traced back to 1950s, with the dawn of recent computers, researchers from different fields began to explore the likelihood of developing computer-aided medical diagnostic (CAD) systems. These early CAD systems used low-charts, statistical pattern-matching, probability theory or knowledge bases to guide their decision-making.

Since the early 1970s, some of the earliest CAD systems in medicine, often called "expert systems", have been developed and used primarily for instructive purposes. (e.g. The MYCIN expert system, the Internist-I expert system and the CADUCEUS expert system).

Throughout the beginning of the primary developments, the researchers aimed to create fully automated CAD/expert systems. Among these scientists, the vision of what these machines could do was unrealistic and optimistic. Nevertheless, after the groundbreaking paper, "Reducibility among combinatorial problems" by Richard M. Karp [1], it became evident that there were drawbacks but also potential opportunities when developing algorithms to unravel groups of significant computer problems. After a modern perception of varied algorithmic limits discovered by Karp within the early 1970s, researchers began to understand the intense limitations of CAD and expert systems in medicine. Recognition of those limitations has led researchers to develop new sorts of CAD systems using advanced approaches. In the late 1980s and early 1990s, the emphasis was placed on using Data Mining approaches to use more sophisticated and scalable CAD systems.

In 1998, the first commercial CAD system for mammography, the ImageChecker system, was approved by the United States Food and Drug Administration (FDA). In the following years, several commercial CAD systems for the analysis of mammography, breast MRI, medical imaging of the lung, colon and heart also received approval from FDA. Currently, CAD systems are used as a diagnostic aid to supply physicians with better medical decision-making [1].

II. CAD Technology

1. Computer-Aided Diagnosis in medical imaging

Computer-Aided diagnosis (CAD) in medical imaging is the use of computer- output as a clinician's assisting tool for making a diagnosis (Figure 1). It is distinct from automated computer diagnosis, where the final diagnosis is based solely on a computer algorithm.

For several years, computer-aided diagnostic systems have been widely used within radiology as an early example of artificial intelligence. The most popular applications are in mammography for breast cancer diagnosis and in chest CT 3 for pulmonary nodules. These programs have historically focused on manual feature engineering based on domain knowledge, but more recent methods employ machine learning to uncover latent features within imaging data. The word CAD is often commonly used for both computer-aided detection and computer-aided diagnosis:

> ➤ Computer-Aided Detection (CADe): Marks different picture areas that may appear irregular, intended to reduce the possibility of overlooking interesting pathologies.

> ➤ Computer-Aided Diagnosis (CADx): assists a doctor in evaluating and classifying pathology in medical imaging.

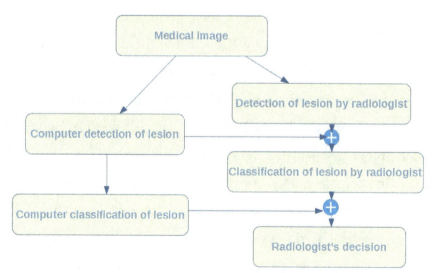

Figure 1: Computer-Aided Diagnosis for medical images

2. The workflow of CAD

A typical CAD system usually follows a five-stages approach during its development phase. These steps are ordered as follows: Data pre-processing, segmentation, features extraction /selection, features classification and detection lesions if we're in CADe system (Figure 2) whereas tendency of malignancy if we're in CADx system (Figure 3).

A more general system is represented in figure 4.

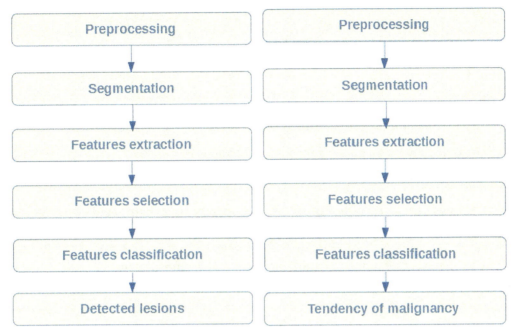

Figure 2: General scheme of CADe   **Figure 3:** General scheme of CADx

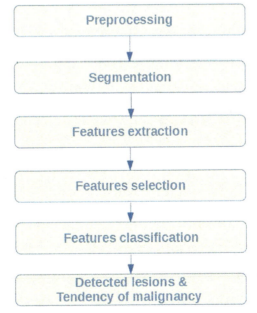

Figure 4: General scheme of CAD

a) Pre-processing

Image preprocessing is the set of operations performed on an image; either to enhance it or to restore it, i.e. to reproduce the original signal. Such preprocesses consist, on the one hand, of changing the appearance of an image so that an information can be easily retrieved, and, on the other hand, of eliminating an irrelevant information (noise) from the images to reinforce the one that is useful for further processing, the result of classification will depend surely on the image quality. Here are the different methods used in preprocessing [2]:

➤ Editing histograms,

➤ Dynamic extension, cropping: Enhancement of gray levels, Masking areas, and Histogram equalization,

➤ Noise reduction in an image: Mean filter, Gaussian filter, and Median Filter,

➤ Edge Detection: The Gradient method, and Laplacian approach.

b) Segmentation

An image's segmentation is a partition of the image into homogeneous pixel sets (according to a predefined criterion) in order to distinguish between the region of interest and the background. The segmentation is not unique (algorithms, homogeneity criterion, initialization, etc.) [3]:

Homogeneity criteria:

➤ Grayscale segmentation,

➤ Color segmentation,

➤ Texture segmentation,

➤ Edges segmentation.

c) Features extraction

After a segmenting and preprocessing operations to adequate the images, features extraction is required. Feature extraction in image processing is a method of transforming large redundant data into a reduced data representation. Transforming the input data into the set of features is called feature extraction [4]:

➤ Fractal Dimension,

➤ Local Binary Patterns(LBP),

➤ Texture Features,

- ➤ Shape Features,
- ➤ Color Feature.

d) Features selection

Variable selection and Attribute selection are other terms for feature selection. It is essentially the selection of a subset of accessible features from a broader pool of accessible features. It is, in other words, the process of picking the most important/relevant characteristics for subsequent categorization. There are two major types of algorithms for feature selection: wrapper methods, and filter methods [5]:

- ➤ Wrapper Feature Selection Methods,
- ➤ Filter Feature Selection Methods.

e) Features classification

A features vector will conveniently represent a collection of numeric features.

One-way binary classification can be accomplished by using a linear predictor function (related to the perception) with a feature vector as input. The procedure consists of measuring the scalar product between the characteristic vector and a weight vector, comparing the result with a threshold and evaluating the class on the basis of this comparison [6]. Classifiers from a feature vector include:

- ➤ Linear classifiers,
- ➤ Non-linear classifiers: Quadratic classifier, Bayesian classifier, Neural networks, SVM, and N nearest neighbors...ext.

III. CAD applications:

CAD is used in the diagnosis of breast cancer, lung cancer, colon cancer, prostate cancer, bone metastases, coronary artery disease, congenital heart defect, pathological brain detection, Alzheimer's disease, and diabetic retinopathy [7].

Conclusion

In this chapter, I introduced the CAD architecture and its application areas. In the next chapter, I will cover the key principals of images classification.

Chapter 2: Images Classification

Introduction

Images classification consists on assigning images from a set of data to predefined categories or classes. In this chapter, I will introduce the most known classification methods and which refer to the existence of groups or classes of data, they are divided into two categories: Classification and Clustering.

In machine learning, two pattern detection procedures are used: classification and clustering. Although the similitude of both techniques, the difference lies in the fact that classification uses predefined classes for assigning images. However, clustering detects similarities between images and groups them based on particular properties. Such groups are called: Clusters.

I will present these different methods further by highlighting classification in supervised learning.

I.   Classification and Clustering

Both classification and clustering are used to categorize objects into one or more classes depending on their functionality. They seem to be similar processes since the fundamental difference is small.

1. Classification

Classification is defined as a supervised learning technique; it is similar to categorization. Classification is a process in which mathematical models are equipped to allocate new findings to a "class" from a set of candidate classes. The models are able to classify new data through analyzing the classification of previous cases. It is a two-step process, involving a learning phase and a classification phase (Figure 5). Some algorithms for classification are:

> Neural Network

> Decision Tree

> K-nearest nighbors (KNN)

> Support Vector Machines (SVM)

> Random Forest

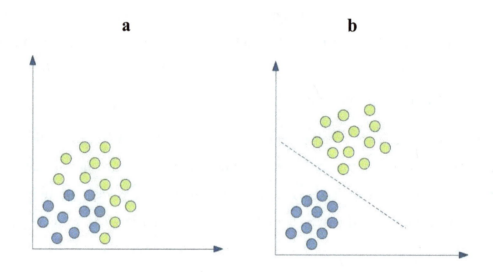

Figure 5: Classification in machine learning

2. Clustering

Clustering is defined as an unsupervised learning technique, it is a method in data analysis. It aims to divide a collection of data into different homogeneous "packets", in the sense that the data of each subset share common characteristics, which most often correspond to proximity criteria that we define by introducing classes and distance measures between objects (Figure 6).

Some algorithms for clustering are:

- ➢ K-means.
- ➢ Hierarchical Clustering.
- ➢ DBSCAN.

a   b

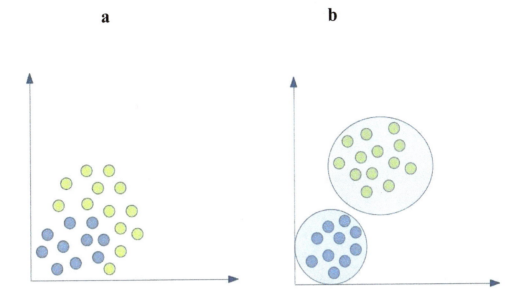

Figure 6: Clustering in machine learning

2. Comparison between classification and clustering

• Supervision

Their key difference is that clustering is unsupervised and considered as self- learning while classification is supervised since it relies on predefined labels.

• Labeling

Clustering works with unlabeled data, so training is not required. By comparison, in its processes, classification deals with both unlabeled and labeled data.

• Goal

Clustering groups objects together in order to reinforce relations and learn new information from secret patterns while classification helps to decide which object belongs to which group.

• Phases

Clustering usually requires only one phase (grouping), while classification involves two phases, training (the model learns from the training dataset) and testing (the target class is predicted)

- **Prediction**

Classification is more important in prediction compared with clustering because it attempts in particular to identify the target classes.

- **Complexity**

Since the classification consists of several steps, deals with prediction and involves levels, its nature is more complicated compared to clustering which primarily aims at grouping similar attributes.

- **Algorithms**

Clustering algorithms are mainly linear and nonlinear while classification consists of more algorithmic tools such as linear classifiers, **neural networks**, Kernel estimation, decision trees, and support vector machines [8].

Table 1 demonstrates the basic differences between clustering and classification.

Classification	clustering
Supervised learning	Unsupervised learning
Labeled data	Unlabeled data
Verifying where a specific data belongs	Finding similarities among data
Has two phases	Has a single phase
Deals with prediction	Does not generally deal with prediction
More complex	Less complex
Logistic regression, Naive Bayes classifier, Support vector machines etc.	k-means clustering algorithm, Fuzzy c-means clustering algorithm, Gaussian (EM) clustering algorithm etc.

Table 1: Classification versus Clustering

II.   Machine Learning: Supervised and Unsupervised Learning

1.   Machine Learning

In principle, machines, computers and programs only function the way you have previously configured them: "if case A occurs, trigger B". However, our expectations of modern computer systems are increasing and the programs cannot foresee every conceivable case and impose a solution on the computer. It is therefore necessary for the software to make autonomous decisions and react appropriately to unknown situations. But algorithms must be available to allow programs to learn. This means that it must first be fed with data and that it can then make associations "**Learn**".

There're two known methods in machine learning: supervised learning and unsupervised learning. I will focus on the first methods in the following:

a)   Supervised Learning

In essence, developers differentiate with incremental intermediate steps supervised learning and unsupervised learning. The algorithms employed are very different. Supervised learning brings examples, such as a database, to the system. Developers specify the value of information, for example, whether it belongs to category A or B (Figure 7). The machine learning system draws conclusions, recognizes patterns and can better handle unknown data. The goal is to further reduce the error rate.

- Mathematical presentation:

    Annotated examples of data are given: (x_1, y_1), (x_2, y_2), (x_3, y_3) … and we predict the output on new data: $x^* \longrightarrow y^*$.

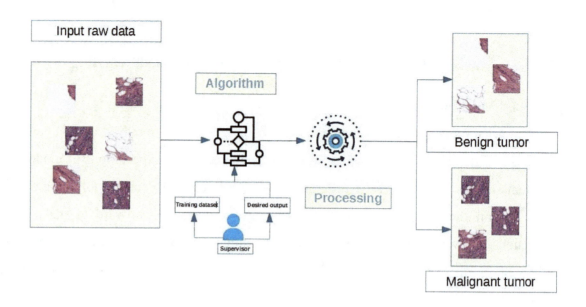

Figure 7: Supervised Learning

b) Unsupervised Learning

Unsupervised learning excludes the instructor, who often suggests what belongs in supervised learning, and provides feedback on autonomous system decisions. Instead, the program here tries to recognize the patterns by itself (Figure 8). It can use clustering (partitioning of data), for example: an element is selected from the quantity of data, examined for its characteristics and then compared with those already examined. If it has already examined equivalent elements, the current object will be added to it. If not, then it is stored separately.

- Mathematical presentation:

  Only raw observations of random variables are given: x_1, x_2, x_3, x_4.... and we expect the deduction of the relation: $x_i \longrightarrow y_i$.

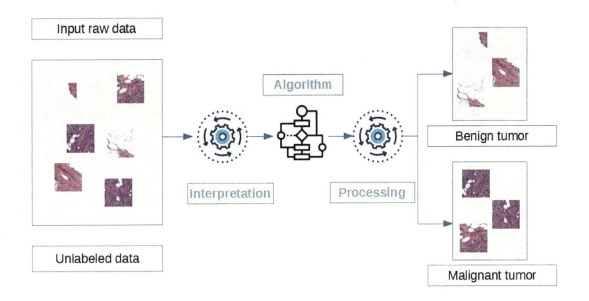

Figure 8: Unsupervised Learning

In addition to these two approaches, there is also semi-supervised learning, reinforcement learning, and active learning (Figure 9).

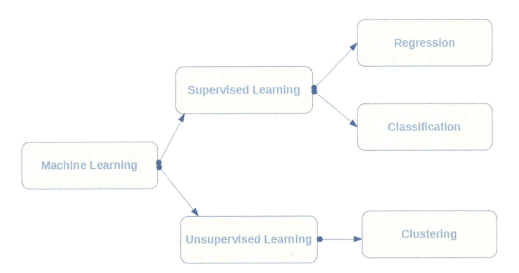

Figure 9: Fundamental approaches in Machine Learning

# III.	Supervised Machine Learning

## 1.	Classification in supervised learning

In this work, I will focus on classification in supervised learning. As was discussed earlier, supervised learning includes two categories of algorithms: regression and classification. Classification is in its turn divided into two other categories:

- **Binary classification:**

This involves classifying the input of a given set into two groups, i.e. predicting which group each variable belongs to. Problems like predicting whether an image represents a malignant tumor or a benign tumor is a binary classification problem.

- **Multi-class classification:**

If there are more than two outputs to a classification problem, it is called a multi-class classification. Problems like predicting whether an image represents sarcoma of the breast, metaplastic carcinoma, adenocystic carcinoma, phyllodes tumor or angiosarcomais is a multi-class classification problem.

## 2.	Classification algorithms:

- **Neural Network:**

As showed in Figure 10, neural network is represented as a directed graph whose nodes correspond to neurons and edges correspond to links between them. Each neuron receives as input a weighted sum of the outputs of the neurons connected to its incoming edges. It has various use cases. An example is in Computer Vision which is done **through Convolutional Neural Networks (CNN).**

- **K-NN:**

Nearest Neighbor algorithms are among the simplest of all machine learning algorithms. The idea is to memorize the training set and then to predict the label of any new instance on the basis of the labels of its closest neighbors in the training set. The rationale behind such a method is based on the assumption that the features that are used to describe the domain points are relevant to their labeling in a way that makes close-by points likely to have the same label. Furthermore, in some situations, even when the training set is immense, finding a nearest neighbor can be done extremely fast [10]. One of the biggest use cases of K-NN search is in the development of Recommender Systems (Figure 11).

- **Decision Tree:**

A decision tree is a predictor, h: $X \rightarrow Y$, that predicts the label associated with an instance x by traveling from a root node of a tree to a leaf. For simplicity we focus on the binary classification setting, namely, $Y = \{0;1\}$, but decision trees can be applied for other prediction problems as well. At each node on the root-to-leaf path, the successor child is chosen on the basis of a splitting of the input space. Usually, the splitting is based on one of the features of x or on a predefined set of splitting rules (Figure 12) [10].

- **Random Forests:**

Random forest, as its name implies, is made up of a large number of individual decision trees which act as an ensemble. Every single tree in the random forest spits out a class prediction and the class with the most votes is the prediction of our model.

- **Super Vector Machines:**

A support vector machine (SVM) can be imagined as a surface that maximizes the boundaries between various types of points of data that is represent in multidimensional space, also known as a hyperplane, which creates the most homogeneous points in each sub region. Support vector machines can be used on any type of data, but have special extra advantages for data types with very high dimensions relative to the observations. For example: For the quality control of DNA sequencing by labeling chromatograms correctly [11].

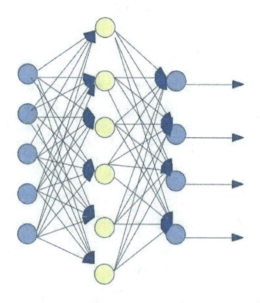

Figure 10: Artificial Neural Network

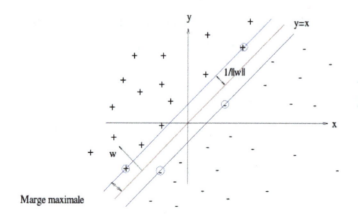

Figure 11: support vector machine

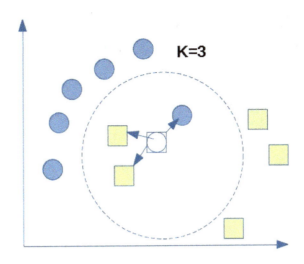

Figure 12: K Nearest Neighbors

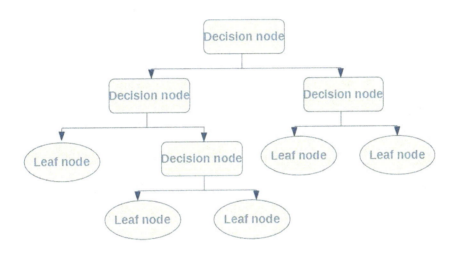

Figure 13: Decision Tree

Conclusion

In this chapter, I presented the basic categorization approaches "clustering and classification", focused on classification in supervised learning for its importance in the coming chapters; as I defined the most popular algorithms in classification. In the next chapter, I will introduce artificial neural networks and deep learning and explain the most crucial concepts.

Chapter 3: Convolutional neural networks and Deep Learning

Introduction

The ML algorithms described in the first part work well for a wide variety of problems. However, they failed to solve some major Artificial Intelligence (AI) problems such as speech recognition and object recognition.

Deep Learning (DL) is based on the idea of artificial neural networks and is conceived to handle large amounts of data by adding layers to the network. A deep learning model has the ability to extract characteristics from raw data thanks to the multiple processing layers composed of multiple linear and non-linear transformations and learn about these characteristics gradually through each layer with minimal human intervention.

One of the fundamental differences between DL and traditional ML algorithms is that the more data you provide, the better the performance of a Deep Learning algorithm is. As they are even able to exceed human performance in areas like image processing.

In this chapter, I will present the concepts related to Deep Learning and artificial neural networks.

I. Deep Learning

Deep learning is a subfield of machine learning that is based on a specific sort of learning process. It is distinguished by the endeavor to develop a learning model at many levels, with the most profound layers taking as input the outputs of the lower ones, altering them, and constantly abstracting more. This understanding of learning levels is motivated by the way the brain processes information and learns in response to external stimuli. Each learning level corresponds, in theory, to one of the several regions that comprise the cerebral cortex.

Table 2 demonstrates the difference between Machine Learning and Deep Learning.

Machine Learning	Deep Learning
Originated around 1960s	Originated around 1970s
A practice getting machines to make decisions without being programmed	The process of using Artificial Neural Networks to solve complex problems
A subset of AI and Data Science	A subset of Machine Learning ,AI and Data Science
Aim is to make machines learn through data so that they can solve problems	Aim is to build Neural Networks that automatically discover patterns for feature detection

Table 2: ML versus DL

II.   History of ANN

In [12], the history of ANNs is summarized as follows:

1957: proposal of the perceptron by Frank Rosenblatt

1967: demonstration by Marvin Minsky that the perceptron is unable to process non-linearly separable data, disinterested in neural approaches.

1986: Rumelhart, Hinton and Williams demonstrate the use of gradient propagation for training the multilayer perceptron.

1995-2005: development of SVM, loss of interest for neural networks.

2006: first deep architectures of neural networks.

2012: Object Recognition (Toronto, ImageNet) and Speech (Microsoft) demonstrate the potential of disruptive deep learning technology.

2014: explosion of private investments in machine learning, in particular in deep learning.

III. Biological neuron

A nerve cell (neuron) is a biological specific cell that processes information. There are large numbers of neurons, about 10^{11} with various interconnections, about 10^{15} according to an estimation (Figure 13).

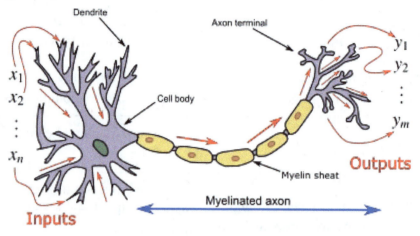

Figure 14: the biological neuron

1. Working of a Biological Neural

As shown in figure 13, a typical neuron consists of the following four sections with the aid of which we can illustrate how it works [13]:

- **Dendrites***:* They are tree-like branches responsible for receiving information from the other neurons to which they are connected.

- **Soma***:* It is the neuron's cell nucleus, which is responsible for information processing, which they have obtained from dendrites.

- **Axon***:* It is like a cable where information is sent through by neurons.

- **Synapses***:* It's the link between the axon and other neuronal dendrites.

2. AN VS BN

Consider the terminology-based similarities between artificial neuron (AN) and the biological neuron (BN), before looking at the differences.

Biological Neural (BN)	Artificial Neural Network (AN)
Soma	Node
Dendrites	Input
Synapse	Weights or Interconnections
Axon	Output

Table 3: Similarities between BN and AN

IV. Artificial Neural Network:

The artificial neuron, like the biological neuron, is made up of the following components:

- One or more incoming connections tasked with gathering numerical signals from other neurons; each connection is allocated a weight that will be used to evaluate each delivered signal.

- One or more output connections that deliver the signal to the remaining neurons.

- An activation function calculates the numerical value of the output based on signals received from input connections with other neurons, as well as the weights related to each picked-up signal and therefore the neuron's own activation threshold. [14].

The following figure represents the artificial neuron (Figure 14):

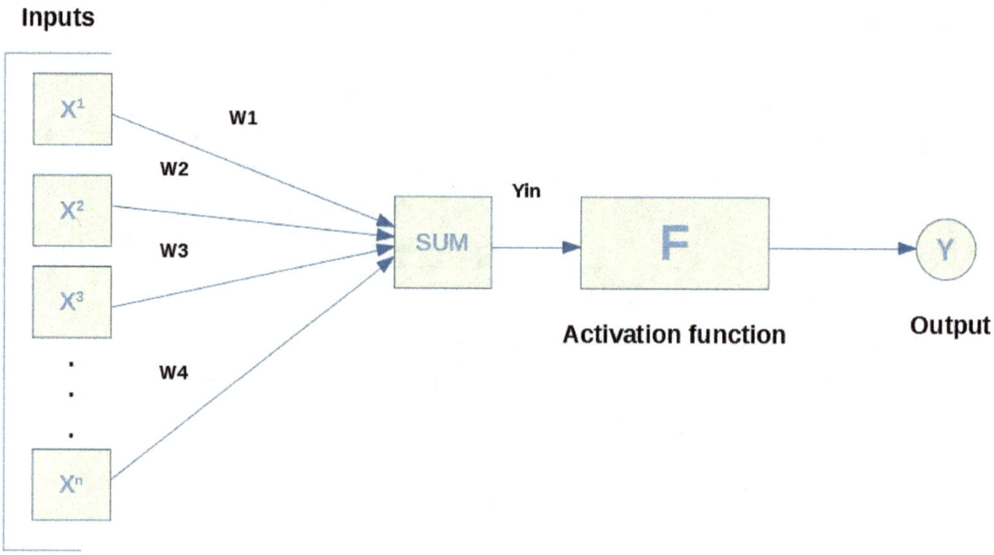

Figure 15: General model of AN

Inputs (x_1, x_2, x_3, ..., x_n)

Weights (w_1, w_2, w_3, ..., w_n)

For the general artificial neural network model above, the net input is calculated as follows:

$$y_{in} = x_1 * w_1 + x_2 * w_2 + x_3 * w_3 + ... + x_n * w_m$$

$$\text{Input } y_{in} = \sum x_i * w_i$$

The activation function applied to the net input can be used to determine the output.

$$Y = F(y_{in})$$

Output = function (net input calculated)

I.   ANN building

Processing of ANN depends upon the following three building blocks:

- Network Topology.
- Adjustments of Weights or Learning.
- Activation Functions.

1. **Network Topology**

A network topology is the arrangement of a network with its connecting nodes and lines. ANN may be categorized as

the following categories according to the topology:

a) **Feedback Network**

This kind of network is characterized by the power to let information recursively circulate partially or completely. It is divisible into the following types:

- **Recurrent networks:** They are closed-loop feedback networks. The next two forms of recurrent networks follow.

    - **Fully recurrent network:** This is the simplest architecture of the neural network, since all nodes are connected to all other nodes and each node acts as both input and output.

    - **Jordan network:** It is a closed loop network in which the output goes as feedback to the input again.

b) **Feedforward Network**

Feedforward Network quite simply means that the data crosses the input-output network without going backwards. Typically, in the family of forward propagation networks, a distinction is made between monolayer networks (simple perceptron) and multilayer networks (multilayer perceptron)

- **Single layer feedforward network:** The simple perceptron is said to be simple because it has only two layers; the input layer and the output layer. The network is triggered by the receipt of input information. The data processing in this network is done between the input layer and the output layer that are all linked together. The entire network thus only has a weight matrix. Having a single weight matrix limits the simple perceptron to a linear classifier that divides the set of information obtained into two distinct categories.

- **Multilayer feedforward network:** The multilayer perceptron is structured in the same way. Information comes in through an input layer and exit through an output layer. Unlike the simple perceptron, the multilayer perceptron has one or more so-called "hidden" layers between the input layer and the output layer. The number of layers corresponds to the numbers of weight matrices available to the network. A multilayer perceptron is therefore better suited to handle the types of non-linear functions.

2. Adjustments of Weights or Learning

The process of altering the weights of connections between the neurons of a defined network is known as learning in artificial neural networks. In ANN, there are three types of learning: supervised learning, unsupervised learning, and reinforcement learning. But in this section, I will be covering supervised learning only.

Supervised Learning: is a system that provides both input data and expected output data. Input and output data are labeled for classification to establish a learning base for further processing of the data. The input vector is introduced to the network during the training of ANN under supervised learning which will provide an output vector.

On the basis of comparison of this output vector with the intended output vector, if there is a disparity between the real output and the desired output vector an error signal is produced. The weights are modified on the basis of this error signal until the final output matches with the desired output (Figure15).

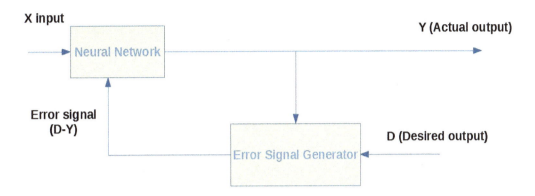

Figure 16: ANN: Supervised Learning

1. **Activation Functions**

An artificial neuron calculates a "weighted sum" of its input, adds a bias and then decides whether the neuron should be activated or not.

$$Y=\sum (weight* \ input + Bias)$$

There is a set of activation functions that differs in complexity and output:

- **Rectified linear unit (ReLU):**

This function converges faster, optimizes and produces the desired value faster. It is by far the most popular activation function used in hidden layers (Figure 16).

$$R(Z) = \max(0, Z)$$

- **Sigmoid:**

The sigmoid function takes a real value as input and returns a number between 0 and 1. It has a set output range and is non-linear, continuously differentiable, monotonic, and non-linear. (Figure 16).

$$\sigma(Z) = \frac{1}{1 + \exp(-Z)}$$

- **Softmax:**

Used in the output layer because it reduces dimensions and can represent a categorical distribution.

$$\sigma(z)_j = \frac{e^{z_j}}{\sum_{k=1}^{k} e^{z_k}} \; for \; j = 1, \dots, k$$

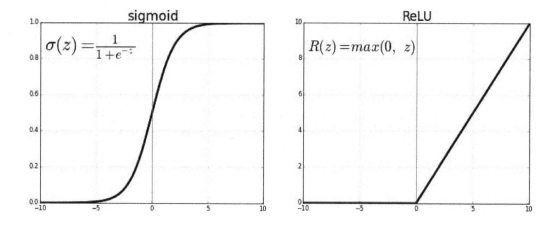

Figure 17: ANN: ReLU vs Sigmoid

II.   Backpropagation

The concept of backpropagation helps neural networks to improve their accuracy. In traditional software applications, a number of functions are coded. These functions take input values and produce an output value. Entries are not used to update instruction.

However, neural networks are artificially intelligent. In the sense that they can learn and improve. When neural networks are formed, a range of input values is transmitted with the corresponding expected output value. The activation functions then produce an output from all of the inputs.

Back propagation: helps the neural network to learn

When the actual result is different from the expected result, the weights applied to the neurons are updated. Sometimes the expected and actual results are within the error threshold and the neural network is considered optimal.

However, the expected output is sometimes different from the actual output. As a result, information is returned to the network and the weights and biases are improved. This process is recursive in nature and is called back propagation.

The back-propagation process allows algorithms to self-learn. Thus, back propagation makes neural networks intelligent by automatically improving.

V. Types of ANN

There are different types of neural networks. The two most popular neural networks are:

- Recurrent Neural Network (RNN): save the results produced by the processing nodes and feed the model using these results. This learning mode is a little more complex.

- Convolution Neural Network (CNN): are increasingly used in various fields: facial recognition, text scanning, natural language processing.

VI. Convolutional neural networks (CNN)

In 2012, during the annual ILSVRC (ImageNet Large Scale Visual Recognition Challenge) computer vision competition, a new Deep Learning algorithm exploded the records. It was a Convolutional Neural Network (CNN) called AlexNet. CNNs have a similar methodology to that of traditional supervised learning methods: they receive input images, detect the features of each of them, then train a classifier on them. However, features are learned automatically. The CNNs themselves do all the tedious work of extracting and describing features: during the training phase, the classification error is minimized in order to optimize the parameters of the classifier and the features. In addition, the specific architecture of the network makes it possible to extract features of different complexities, from the simplest to the most sophisticated. One of the strengths of CNNs is the automatic extraction and hierarchy of features, which adapt to the given problem: no need to implement an extraction algorithm "by hand", like SIFT (Scale-invariant Feature Transform) or Harris- Stephens. Unlike supervised learning techniques, CNNs learn the features of each image. Therein lies their strength: networks do all the job of extracting features automatically, unlike learning techniques.

Today, CNNs, also called ConvNet, are still the most efficient models for the classification of images. This part is therefore naturally devoted to them.

1. Difference between ANN and CNN

CNNs designate a subcategory of neural networks: they therefore have all the characteristics listed in the previous chapter. However, CNNs are specially designed to process input images. Their architecture is then more specific: it is composed of two main blocks (Figure 17).

The first block "Convolutional base" is the particularity of this type of neural network, since it functions as a feature extractor. To do this, it performs template matching by applying convolution-filtering operations. The first layer filters the image with several convolution kernels, and returns "feature maps", which are then normalized (with an activation function) and / or resized. This process can be repeated several times: we filter the feature maps obtained with new kernels, which gives us new feature maps to normalize and resize, and that we can filter again, and so on. Finally, the values of the last feature maps are concatenated into a vector. This vector defines the output of the first block, and the input of the second.

The second block "**Classifier**" is not characteristic of a CNN: it is in fact found at the end of all the neural networks used for classification. The values of the input vector are transformed (with several linear combinations and activation functions) to return a new vector as output. This last vector contains as many elements as there are classes: element i represents the probability that the image belongs to class i. Each element is therefore between 0 and 1, and the sum of all is 1. These probabilities are calculated by the last layer of this block (and therefore of the network), which uses a logistic function (binary classification) or a Softmax function (multi-class classification) as an activation function.

As with ordinary neural networks, the parameters of the layers are determined by backpropagation of the gradient: cross entropy is minimized during the training phase. But in the case of CNNs, these parameters designate in particular the features of the images [14].

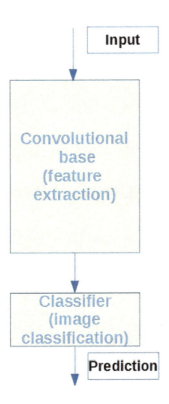

Figure 18: Architecture of a model based on CNN.

1. The different layers of a CNN

There are four types of layers for a convolutional neural network: the convolution layer, the pooling layer, the ReLU correction layer and the fully-connected layer. I will explain how these different layers work (Figure 18).

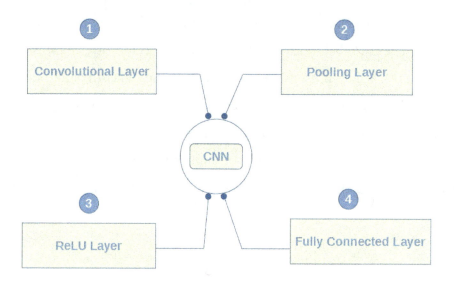

Figure 19: CNN Layers

a) The convolutional layer

The convolutional layer is the key component of CNNs and always constitutes at least their first layer.

Its purpose is to identify the presence of a set of features in the images received as input. To do this, we perform convolution filtering: the principle is to "drag" a window representing the feature on the image, and calculate the convolution product between the feature and each portion of the scanned image (Figure 19). A feature is then seen as a filter.

$$(I*h)[x,y]=\sum_{i=x_1}^{x_2}\sum_{j=y_1}^{y_2}h[i,j]\cdot I[x-i,y-j]$$

Where I is a 2D image and h is the kernel performed on the image.

The convolution layer therefore receives as input several images and calculates the convolution of each of them with each filter. The filters correspond exactly to the features that we want to find in the images.

We obtain for each pair (image, filter) an activation map, or feature map, which tells us where the features are in the image: the higher the value, the more the corresponding place in the image looks like the feature.

Unlike traditional methods, features are not pre-defined according to a particular formalism (for example SIFT), but learned by the network during the training phase. The filter cores designate the weights of the convolution layer. These weights are initialized and then updated by backpropagation of the gradient.

This is the strength of CNNs: these are capable of determining the discriminating elements of an image on their own, by adapting to the problem posed. For example, if the question is to distinguish cats from dogs, the automatically defined features can describe the shape of the ears or legs [15].

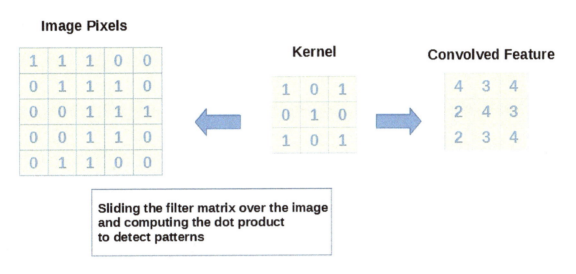

Figure 20: Convolution filter

a) **The pooling layer**

This type of layer is often placed between two convolutional layers: it receives several feature maps as input, and applies the pooling operation to each of them.

The pooling operation consists in reducing the size of the images, while preserving their important characteristics.

For this, we cut the input into regular cells, then we keep within each cell the maximum value. In practice, small square cells are often used so as not to lose too much information. The most common choices are adjacent cells of size 2 × 2 pixels which do not overlap, or cells of size 3 × 3 pixels, spaced from each other by a step of 2 pixels (which therefore overlap). We get the same number of feature maps as the input, but much smaller (Figure 20).

The pooling layer makes it possible to reduce the number of parameters and calculations in the network. This improves the efficiency of the network and avoids over-fitting.

Maximum values are less accurately identified in feature maps obtained after pooling than in those received as input - this is actually a big advantage. For example, when you want to recognize a dog, its ears do not need to be located as precisely as possible: knowing that they are located almost next to the head is enough.

Thus, the pooling layer makes the network less sensitive to the position of features: the fact that a feature is a little higher or lower, or even that it has a slightly different orientation should not cause a radical change in the classification of the image [16].

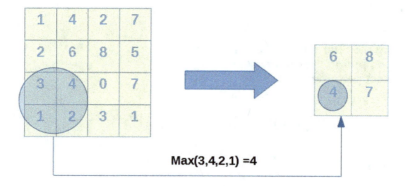

Figure 21: The Pooling operation

a) The ReLU correction layer

ReLU (Rectified Linear Units) designates the real non-linear function defined by ReLU f(x) = max (0, x), (Figure 21).

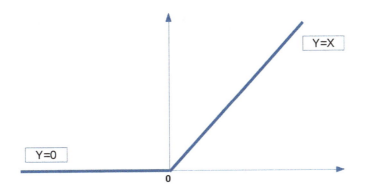

Figure 22: ReLU function

The ReLU correction layer therefore replaces all negative values received as inputs with zeros. It plays the role of activation function (Figure 22).

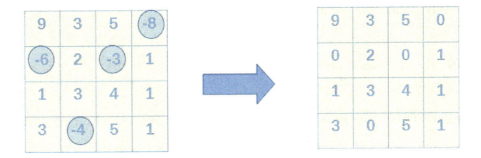

Figure 23: ReLU applied

b) The fully-connected layer

The fully-connected layer is always the last layer of a neural network, convolutional or not. It is therefore not characteristic of a CNN.

This type of layer receives an input vector and produces a new output vector (Figure 23). To do this, it applies a linear combination and then optionally an activation function to the values received as input.

The last fully-connected layer makes it possible to classify the image at the input of the network: it returns a vector of size N, where N is the number of classes in our image classification problem. Each element of the vector indicates the probability for the input image to belong to a class.

For example, if the problem consists in distinguishing cats from dogs, the final vector will be of size 2: the first element (respectively, the second) gives the probability of belonging to the class "cat" (respectively "dog"). Thus, the vector [0.9, 0.1] means that the image has a 90% chance of representing a cat.

Each value in the input table "votes" in favor of a class. The votes do not all have the same importance: the layer gives them weights which depend on the element of the table and the class.

To calculate the probabilities, the fully-connected layer therefore multiplies each input element by a weight, makes the sum, then applies an activation function (logistics if $N = 2$, softmax if $N > 2$): This processing amounts to multiplying the input vector by the matrix containing the weights. The fact that each input value is connected with all output values explains the term fully-connected (Figure 24).

The convolutional neural network learns the values of the weights in the same way that it learns the filters of the convolution layer: during the training phase, by backpropagation of the gradient.

The fully-connected layer determines the link between the position of features in the image and a class. Indeed, the input table being the result of the previous layer, it corresponds to an activation card for a given feature: high values indicate the location (more or less precise depending on the pooling) of this feature in the image. If the location of a feature at a certain place in the image is characteristic of a certain class, then we give significant weight to the corresponding value in the table [17].

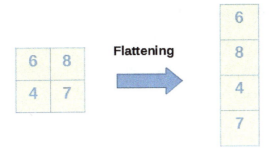

Figure 24: Flattening operation

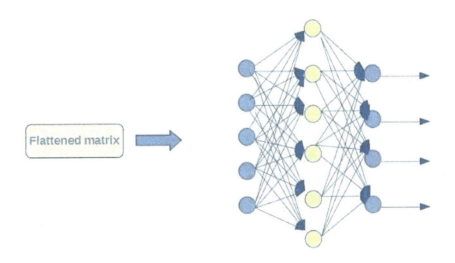

Figure 25: Fully-Connected layer

1. Architecture of a convolutional neural network

A CNN is simply a stack of several layers of convolution, pooling, ReLU correction and fully-connected. Each image received as input will therefore be filtered, reduced and corrected several times, finally forming a vector. In the classification problem, this vector contains the probabilities of belonging to classes.

All convolutional neural networks must start with a convolutional layer and end with a fully-connected layer. Intermediate layers can be stacked in different ways, provided that the output from a layer has the same structure as the input of the next one. For example, a fully-connected layer, which always returns a vector, cannot be placed before a pooling layer, since the latter must receive a 3D matrix.

In general, a neural network stacks several layers of convolution and ReLU correction, then optionally adds a pooling layer and repeats this pattern several times; then, it stacks fully-connected layers. The more layers, the deeper the neural network: Deep Learning.

The first convolution layer learns simple features, which represent rudimentary structural elements of the image (edges, corners ...). The higher the convolution layers, that is to say far from the input of the network, the more complex the learned features: these consist of the simpler features of the previous layers. A square is an example of a complex feature, consisting of edges and corners.

The highest convolutional layers therefore learn sophisticated features: for example, in the case of the dog / cat classification, they can correspond to the ears or the legs (Figure 25).

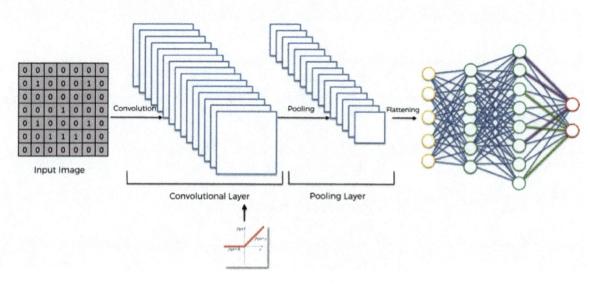

Figure 26: Convolutional Neural Networks

1. The configuration of the layers

A CNN is distinguished from another by the way the layers are stacked, but also configured.

The convolution and pooling layers have hyperparameters, that is, parameters whose value must be defined beforehand.

The features of the convolutional layer and the weights of the fully-connected layer are not hyperparameters, since they are learned by the neural network during the training phase.

The size of the feature maps output from the convolution and pooling layers depends on the hyperparameters.

Each image (or feature map) has dimensions $W \times H \times D$, where W is its width in pixels, H its height in pixels and D the number of channels (1 for a black and white image, 3 for a colors).

The convolution layer has four hyperparameters:

1. The number of filters K.
2. The size F of the filters: the dimensions of each filter are $F \times F \times D$ pixels.
3. Step S with which we drag the window corresponding to the filter on the image. For example, a step of 1 means that the window is moved one pixel at a time.
4. The zero-padding P: we add to the image at the input of the layer a padding with P pixels. Without this, the output dimensions are smaller. Thus, the more convolution layers are stacked with P = 0, the more the image at the input of the network shrinks. So, we lose a lot of information quickly which makes the task of extracting features difficult.

For each image of size W × H × D at input, the convolution layer returns a matrix of dimensions WC × HC × DC , where WC = ((W − F + 2P) /S)+ 1, HC = ((H − F + 2P) /S)+ 1 and DC = K.

Choosing P = (F − 1) /2 and S = 1 thus makes it possible to obtain feature maps of the same width and height as those received as input.

The pooling layer has only two hyperparameters:

1. The size F of the cells: the image is divided into square cells of size F × F pixels.

2. Step S: cells are separated from each other by S pixels.

For each image of size W × H × D as input, the pooling layer returns a matrix of dimensions WP × HP × DP, where WP = ((W − F) /S)+ 1, HP = ((H − F) /S)+ 1 and DP = D.

Like stacking, the choice of hyperparameters is done according to a classic scheme:

For the convolution layer, the filters are small and dragged over the image one pixel at a time. The zero-padding value is chosen so that the width and height of the input volume are not changed on output. In general, we then choose F = 3, P = 1, S = 1 or F = 5, P = 2, S = 1.

For the pooling layer, F = 2 and S = 2 is a wise choice. This eliminates 75% of the input pixels. We can also find F = 3 and S = 2: in this case, the cells overlap. Choosing larger cells causes too much information to be lost, and poorer results in practice [18].

5. CNN known models

We now have all the tools to understand the architecture of a convolutional neural network. There are several in the literature whose effectiveness varies according to the task because they do not all have the same number of convolutions (nor the same structure).

These include:

- LeNet (the simplest, to discover the CNN),
- AlexNet (launched in 2012),
- ZFNet (improvement of AlexNet),

- GoogLeNet (parent of the famous Inception, an image recognition algorithmwith other subtleties, just like YOLO, MobileNet, etc.),
- VGGNet (still widely used and powerful),
- ResNet (the same, even if it is different from a traditional CNN).

Conlcusion

In this chapter, I introduced the concept of a neural network (what it is and how it works). In addition, we were able to see an overview of the components that make them artificially intelligent. Finally, I introduced the two most popular types of neural networks, explained how a convolutional neural network works. In particular, I presented the different elements of a CNN architecture (convolutions, pooling, ReLU, flattening, dense ...) and we discovered real networks used in production (ResNet and VGG in particular).

Chapter 4: Application and Implementation

Introduction

This chapter is devoted to the implementation of a CAD system. I will present, in a first place, the development tools used such as Jupyter Notebook, the programming language "Python" and the library Keras.

The second part of this chapter allows the reader to develop models from scratch and exploit pre-trained architectures and datasets used for testing the models.

I.   Development tools

1. Anaconda

Anaconda is a free and open source distribution of Python and R programming languages applied to the development of applications dedicated to data science and machine learning (large-scale data processing, predictive analysis, scientific computing), which aims to simplify package management and deployment. Package versions are managed by the conda package management system (Figure 26). The Anaconda distribution is used by over 19 million users worldwide and includes over 7500 Python/R data science packages suitable for Windows, Linux and MacOS [19].

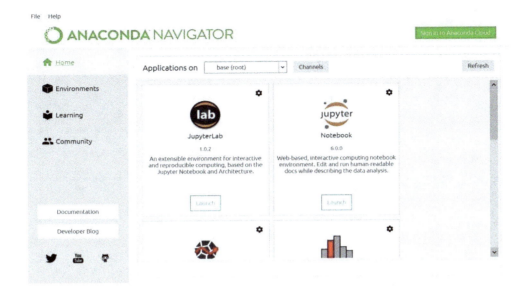

Figure 27: Anaconda distribution

1. Jupyter Notebook

Jupyter notebooks are electronic notebooks that, in the same document, can collect text, images, mathematical formulas and executable computer code (Figure 27). They can be manipulated interactively in a web browser. Initially developed for the Julia, Python and R programming languages (hence the name Jupyter), Jupyter notebooks support nearly 40 different languages.

The cell is the basic element of a Jupyter notebook. It can contain text formatted in Markdown format or computer code that can be executed [20].

Figure 28: Jupyter Notebook interface

1. Python

Python is an interpreted, multi-paradigm and multiplatform programming language. It promotes imperative structured, functional and object-oriented programming. It has strong dynamic typing, automatic memory management by garbage collection and an exception management system; it is thus similar to Perl, Ruby, Scheme, Smalltalk and Tcl. There are many machine learning applications written in Python. Data analysis and data visualization in form of charts can also be developed using Python.

2. Keras

The Keras library makes it possible to interact with the algorithms of deep neural networks and machine learning, in particular Tensorflow, Theano, Microsoft Cognitive Toolkit or PlaidML. Designed to allow rapid experimentation with deep neural networks, it focuses on its ergonomics, its modularity and its expansion capabilities. It was developed as part of the ONEIROS project (Open-ended Neuro- Electronic Intelligent Robot Operating System). It was originally written by François Chollet [21].

II. Datasets and pre-trained models

1. Datasets

a. Invasive Ductal Carcinoma (IDC)

The most prevalent subtype of all breast cancers is Invasive Ductal Carcinoma (IDC). Pathologists often focus on the sections of a whole mount sample that contain the IDC when assigning an aggressiveness grade. As a result, delineating the specific areas of IDC within a whole mount slide is a frequent pre-processing step for automated aggressiveness rating.

162 whole mount slide pictures of Breast Cancer (BCa) specimens were scanned at 40x in the original dataset. 277,524 50 x 50 patches were retrieved from it (198,738 IDC negative and 78,786 IDC positive).

Each patch's file name is of the format (Figure 28):

```
u_xX_yY_classC.png   - > example 10253_idx5_x1351_y1101_class0.png
```

Where u is the patient ID (10253 idx5), X is the x-coordinate of where this patch was cropped from, Y denotes the y-coordinate of where this patch was cropped from, and C is the class, with 0 denoting non-IDC and 1 denoting IDC [22].

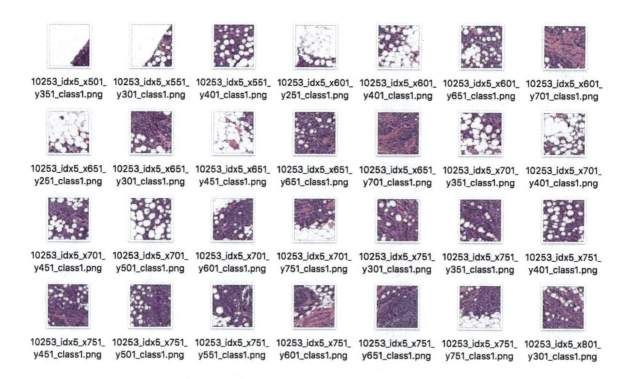

Figure 29: IDC's patches

b) Digital Database for Screening Mammography DDSM

The DDSM database was created by the University of South Florida [25], it's actually widely used in research work related to breast cancer diseases. It consists of 2620 cases of 4 mammograms taken in two views: mediolateral oblique (MLO) and craniocaudal (CC). In each mammogram, suspicious lesions are marked by domain experts and explained by information of ground truth (Figure 29).

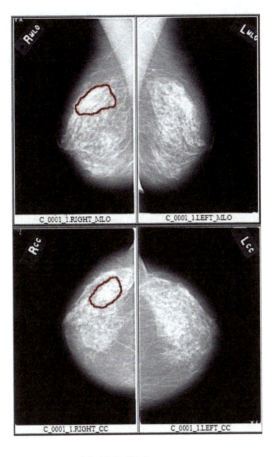

Figure 30: DDSM mammograms

2. Pre-trained models

Models that have been pre-trained on data with varying numbers of classes are known as pre-trained models.

A pre-trained model may not be perfect in every situation, but it saves a lot of time and effort compared to reinventing the wheel.

I will present four pre-trained models from the wide range of pre-trained models that are available in Keras: VGG16, VGG19, DenseNet201, and ResNet50.

a. VGG architecture

- **VGG16**

The layers in VGG16 model are as follows (Figure 30) [23]:

❖ 2 x convolution layer of 64 channel of 3x3 kernel and same padding.

- ❖ 1 x maxpool layer of 2x2 pool size and stride 2x2.

- ❖ 2 x convolution layer of 128 channel of 3x3 kernal and same padding.

- ❖ 1 x maxpool layer of 2x2 pool size and stride 2x2.

- ❖ 3 x convolution layer of 256 channel of 3x3 kernal and same padding.

- ❖ 1 x maxpool layer of 2x2 pool size and stride 2x2.

- ❖ 3 x convolution layer of 512 channel of 3x3 kernel and same padding.

- ❖ 1 x maxpool layer of 2x2 pool size and stride 2x2.

- ❖ 3 x convolution layer of 512 channel of 3x3 kernel and same padding.

- ❖ 1 x maxpool layer of 2x2 pool size and stride 2x2.

- ❖ A relu(Rectified Linear Unit) activation is added to each layers so that all the negative values are not passed to the next layer.

- ❖ 1 x Dense layer of 4096 units.

- ❖ 1 x Dense Softmax layer of 1000 units.

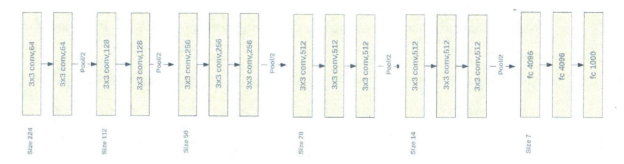

Figure 31: VGG16 architecture

- • **VGG19**

The layers in VGG19 model are as follows (Figure 31):

- ❖ 2 x convolution layer of 64 channel of 3x3 kernel and same padding.
- ❖ 1 x maxpool layer of 2x2 pool size and stride 2x2.
- ❖ 2 x convolution layer of 128 channel of 3x3 kernel and same padding.

- ❖ 1 x maxpool layer of 2x2 pool size and stride 2x2.

- ❖ 4 x convolution layer of 256 channel of 3x3 kernel and same padding.

- ❖ 1 x maxpool layer of 2x2 pool size and stride 2x2.

- ❖ 4 x convolution layer of 512 channel of 3x3 kernel and same padding.

- ❖ 1 x maxpool layer of 2x2 pool size and stride 2x2.

- ❖ 4 x convolution layer of 512 channel of 3x3 kernel and same padding.

- ❖ 1 x maxpool layer of 2x2 pool size and stride 2x2.

- ❖ A relu(Rectified Linear Unit) activation is added to each layers so that all the negative values are not passed to the next layer.

- ❖ 2 x Dense layer of 4096 units.

- ❖ 1 x Dense Softmax layer of 1000 units.

Figure 32: VGG19 architecture

b) ResNet architecture

The Residual Network design introduced a simple but unusual concept: instead of using each constitutional layer's output, blend it with the original input. A simplified version of one of the ResNet modules is shown below; it clearly illustrates the sum operation at the conclusion of the Convolutional layer stack, as well as a final ReLU operation. (Figure 32):

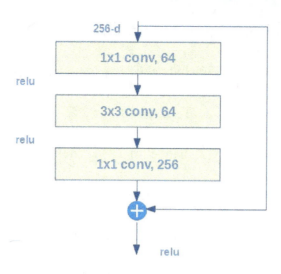

Figure 33: ResNet general architecture

The convolutional part of the module includes a feature reduction from 256 to 64 values, a 3×3 filter layer maintaining the features number, and then a feature augmenting 1×1 layer, from 64 x 256 values. ResNet has recently been employed at a depth of fewer than 30 layers, with a wide distribution [16].

c) DenseNet architecture

Each layer in DenseNet (ResNet Extension) receives extra inputs from all preceding layers and passes on its own feature-maps to all future levels. The term "concatenation" is used. Each layer receives "collective knowledge" from the levels above it.

- **Basic DenseNet Composition Layer**

Perform pre-activation batch normalization (BN) and ReLU for each merge layer, followed by 3x3 conv, with k channel output feature maps. Suppose you want to x_0, x_1, x_2, x_3 to x_4. Pre-Activation ResNet came up with this concept (Figure 33).

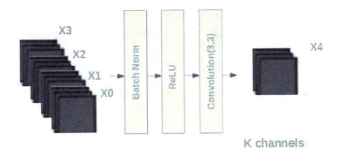

Figure 34: Composition Layer

- **DenseNet-B (Bottleneck Layers)**

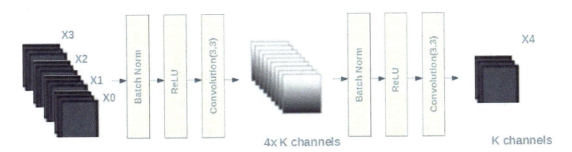

Figure 35: DenseNet-B

BN-ReLU-1x1 Conv is run before BN-ReLU- 3×3 Conv to minimize model complexity and size (Figure 34).

- **Multiple Dense Blocks with Transition Layers**

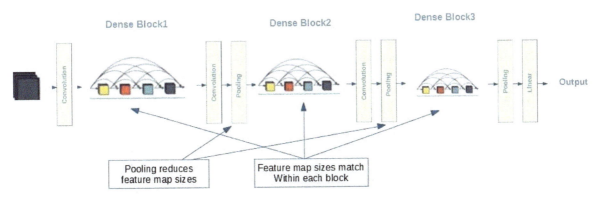

Figure 36: Multiple Dense Blocks

As shown in Figure 35, the transition layers between two continuous dense blocks are 1x1 Conv followed by 2x2 average pooling. Within the dense block, feature map sizes are uniform, allowing them to be readily concatenated. A global average pooling is conducted at the conclusion of the last dense block, and then a Softmax classifier is added. [24].

III.   Ways to Fine tune a pre-trained model

1. **Feature extraction** – We can use a pre-trained model as a feature extraction mechanism. What we can do is that we can remove the output layer and then use the entire network as a fixed feature extractor for the new data set.

2. **Use the Architecture of the pre-trained model** – What we can do is that we use architecture of the model while we initialize all the weights randomly and train the model according to our dataset again.

3. **Train some layers while freeze others** – Another option is to partially train a pre-trained model. What we can do is freeze the weights of the model's first layers while retraining just the upper levels. We may experiment with how many layers to freeze and how many to train (Figure 36).

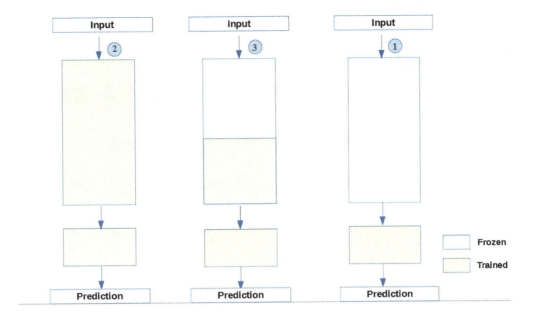

Figure 37: Fine-tuning methods

IV. Implementation

The proposed system includes an anomaly detection phase (Figure 37) and an identification phase (Figure 38).

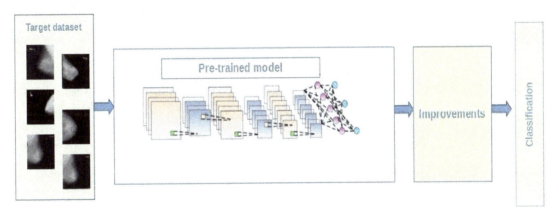

Figure 38: Abstract representation of CADe

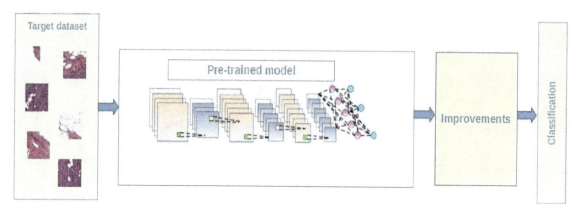

Figure 39: Abstract representation of CADx

On the practical part, we will focus on CADx. Thus, we will build classification models from scratch then exploit the pre-trained model VGG16 with different fine-tuning methods. After understanding this, you will be able to apply other pre-trained models, and also build a CADe only by replacing the path to your data and using DDSM instead of IDC. without further ado, go to google and search for Google Colab.

Google Colaboratory, or Colab, is a simple, free Google tool that introduces you to Deep Learning and helps you collaborate with your colleagues on data science projects.

Colab allows you to:

- Improve your coding skills in the Python programming language.
- Develop deep learning applications using popular Python libraries such as Keras, TensorFlow, PyTorch and OpenCV.
- To use a development environment (Jupyter Notebook) that does not require any configuration.

But the feature that sets Colab apart from other services is access to a GPU graphics processor, completely free of charge.

As the name suggests, Google Colaboratory is accompanied by the term "collaboration". In fact, Colab uses the same collaboration features of other G Suite elements: Sheet, Slide, Docs, etc. It works on Google servers and you don't have to install anything. In addition, Colab documents (Jupyter Notebook) are saved directly to your Google Drive account.

You can use the Jupyter notebook on Anaconda if you want, but don't forget to install all the required libraries. Additionally, for building models from scratch, it is mandatory to possess a good GPU and RAM. On the contrary, I highly recommend you to use Google Colab.

1. Import the IDC dataset from Github to Colab

Open the Colab Notebook and click on connect above then clone the repository on it with one line of code (Figure 40):

! git clone https://github.com/HananeMeftahi0/IDC.git

Figure 40: Clone the IDC repository

2. Libraries

We will use the following libraries to prepare our data:

- Numpy: to manipulate vectors and interact with Keras, our Deep Learning framework. This library is widely used.

- Keras: the deep learning framework. The import of Tensorflow in the backend is done automatically by Keras.

From Keras, we will only take the Tensorflow backend, named K, for which we will specify the input format of the model layers using "th". "Th" means that the kernels of convolutions will have for format (depth, input_depth, rows, cols), unlike "tf" which means (rows, cols, input_depth, depth).

Add the following lines to your file:

```
import numpy as np
from keras.utils import np_utils
from keras import backend as K
K.set_image_data_format('channels_first')
```

We will force the random of numpy: when generating the model, many parameters are chosen randomly by Keras via Numpy. In order to have exactly the same model (and therefore the same results), it is common (IN TUTORIALS ONLY) to set the random with this line (which you must therefore add).

```
seed = 7
np.random.seed(seed)
```

Finally, in Keras we will take this time the model and the layers (convolutions, pooling, etc ...).

```
from keras.models import Sequential
from keras.layers import Dense
from keras.layers import Dropout
from keras.layers import Flatten
from keras.layers.convolutional import Conv2D
from keras.layers.convolutional import MaxPooling2D
```

Other libraries will be added later on this section.

3. Data preparation

We are going to see together how to import the IDC data and, above all, what processing to do before injecting them into our CNN. The "processing" part is usually the most important (and neglected) part in machine learning, because it has a huge impact on AI results.

Let's start by loading the data, which is:

- 8,500 training images (square matrices of size 50 × 50) in RGB (so 3 channels).
- And 1,500 test images (same specifications).

First let's explore data by adding these lines:

```python
from glob import glob
import fnmatch
import cv2
import pandas as pd
imagePatches = glob('/content/IDC/IDC_regular_ps50_idx5
/**/*.png', recursive=True)
patternZero = '*class0.png'
patternOne = '*class1.png'
```

ImagePatches have now the paths to every image in our dataset. PatternZero and patternOne will help us separate images paths into malignant and benign.

```python
classZero = fnmatch.filter(imagePatches, patternZero)
classOne = fnmatch.filter(imagePatches, patternOne)
```

classZero have all the paths to images of class 0 and classOne all the paths to images of class one.

Now all we have to do is retrieve images using the process_images function that takes lowerIndex and upperIndex as parameters. Note that, imagesPatches is an array and each element of an array has its own index (position) starting from zero. So if you write the following array A= [3,5,6,7,8,9] and display only

A [1 : 4] ; you will get only this part of the array [3,5,6,7,8,9] (8 excluded). Now that you know how arrays work, let's proceed. The next step is to read those images via their paths using CV and resize those images using INTER_CUBIC interpolation in order to ensure that all images have the same size, after that all the images are split into their two classes respectively.

```python
def process_images(lowerIndex,upperIndex):

    height = 50
    width = 50
    channels = 3
    x = []
    y = []
    for img in imagePatches[lowerIndex:upperIndex]:

        full_size_image = cv2.imread(img)

        image = (cv2.resize(full_size_image, (width,height),interpolation=cv2.INTER_CUBIC))


        x.append(image)
        if img in classZero:
            y.append(0)

        elif img in classOne:
            y.append(1)
        else:
            return
    return x,y
```

Now call the process_input function using this line of code:

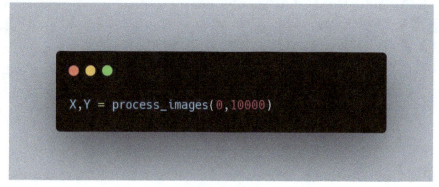

```python
X,Y = process_images(0,10000)
```

X have all the images; and Y has the classes of those images.

We must convert the elements of the matrices to float before dividing by 255 (to have values between 0 and 1). This conversion and normalization is a very important step in the preparation of the data, because it makes it possible to reduce the difference between the extreme values and to avoid overflow in the calculations because numbers greater than 1 can quickly tend towards infinity if we are less careful.

```python
X = np.array(X)
X = X.astype(np.float32)
X /= 255
```

Finally, we can split the data to two sets; one for training and the other for testing using this instruction:

```python
from sklearn.model_selection import train_test_split
X_train, X_test, y_train, y_test = train_test_split(X,Y,test_size=0.15)
```

Then, compared to our "th" configuration of TensorFlow, we will have to slightly modify the structure of the matrices in order for them to be usable in the model.

We currently have 10000x50x50, and we would like 10000x3x50x50 (number of inputs, channels, width, height). The "reshape" command can do exactly that.

```
X_train = X_train.reshape(X_train.shape[0], 3, 50, 50)
X_test = X_test.reshape(X_test.shape[0], 3, 50, 50)
train_test_split(X,Y,test_size=0.15)
```

Finally, last point, we will work on the output vectors so that they reflect the value predicted by the network. Indeed, it would be very complicated to have a CNN that would return one and only one result to us. Conversely, it is easier for a CNN to give us the probability that it is a class zero or class one. This conversion of categorical variables is done easily, thanks to the "one hot encode" system:

```
y_train = np_utils.to_categorical(y_train)
y_test = np_utils.to_categorical(y_test)
num_classes = 2
```

Note that, num_classes represent the number of CNN output values.

4. Build models from scratch

To declare a new deep learning model in Keras, we use the following instruction, which is valid for both ANNs and CNNs as well as anything else:

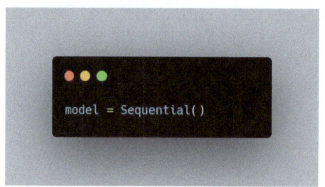

```
model = Sequential()
```

a) Small CNN

Then, the methods to be called are very meaningful. Our objective is to have successively:

- A convolution of 64 filters in 3 × 3 kernel followed by a ReLU activation layer.

- A convolution of 32 filters in 3 × 3 kernel followed by a ReLU activation layer.

- A flatten that will create the final vector to send to the artificial neural network (classifier).

- A dense, artificial neural network that will have 2 neurons and will be followed by a softmax.

Note: softmax is a mathematical function which allows to normalize a vector to make probabilities of it.

To declare a convolution, the syntax is to call Conv2D with as parameters the number of filters, the dimensions of the kernel (3 × 3), specifying input_shape: the size of the input data (only on the 1st layer of the CNN) and finally activation.

Flatten does not take any parameters, because nothing special is needed to put all the images together.

On the other hand, the Dense which is used to declare our artificial neural network takes as a parameter the number of neurons in the output layer, and the "activation" parameter which is here softmax.

you should be able to write the construction of Small CNN:

```python
model.add(Conv2D(64, (3, 3), input_shape=(3, 50, 50), activation='relu'))
model.add(Conv2D(32, (3, 3), activation='relu'))
model.add(Flatten())
model.add(Dense(num_classes, activation='softmax'))
```

Last step in the declaration of our model: it must be compiled via "model.compile" specifying the following information, intrinsic to the convolutional neural network.

- **The loss:** this is a function that will be used to measure the gap between our AI's predictions and the expected results. It therefore assesses the accuracy of the CNN and allows it to better adapt to the data if necessary! We are going to use "categorical_crossentropy" as loss, because we have data of type "categories" at the output of the algorithm.

MEDICAL IMAGES CLASSIFICATION USING DEEP LEARNING

- **The optimizer:** it is an algorithm that will dictate how to update the CNN to decrease the loss, and therefore have better predictions. Here we will rely on "adam" (adaptive moment estimation), very often used.

- **The metrics:** this is exactly like the loss, except that the metrics is NOT used by CNN, unlike the loss which is used for updating CNN variables via the optimizer. This time we will use "accuracy", without this having any real importance for us.

```
model.compile(loss='categorical_crossentropy', optimizer='adam', metrics=['accuracy'])
```

We built our model from start to finish! We just have to start the training. To train a model, all you have to do is call the fit method which takes as arguments:

- The training data, here X_train.

- The expected learning predictions, here y_train.

- The validation_data parameter: a vector that contains the input data to test and the values to predict, here (X_test, y_test).

- The number of iterations, that is, the number of times it will repeat the entire training via epochs. I suggest you put 10.

- And finally the batch_size parameter, which is the number of input data to analyze "consecutively before updating the CNN", which will be equal to 200 (standard value). The advantage is that updating your CNN after each image takes time and tends to move away from the global optimal. By indicating 200, we make sure that the network is not "too specific".

Which gives the following code:

```
model.fit(X_train, y_train, validation_data=(X_test, y_test), epochs=10, batch_size=200)
```

At runtime, you should get a result similar to this one:

```
Epoch 1/10
43/43 [==============================] - 46s 51ms/step - loss: 0.7368 - accuracy: 0.6854 - val_loss: 0.5020 - val_accuracy: 0.7133
Epoch 2/10
43/43 [==============================] - 1s 31ms/step - loss: 0.4467 - accuracy: 0.7676 - val_loss: 0.4266 - val_accuracy: 0.7967
Epoch 3/10
43/43 [==============================] - 1s 33ms/step - loss: 0.3422 - accuracy: 0.8561 - val_loss: 0.3186 - val_accuracy: 0.8647
Epoch 4/10
43/43 [==============================] - 1s 32ms/step - loss: 0.3094 - accuracy: 0.8773 - val_loss: 0.3039 - val_accuracy: 0.8707
Epoch 5/10
43/43 [==============================] - 1s 31ms/step - loss: 0.3015 - accuracy: 0.8802 - val_loss: 0.2966 - val_accuracy: 0.8760
Epoch 6/10
43/43 [==============================] - 1s 31ms/step - loss: 0.2904 - accuracy: 0.8811 - val_loss: 0.2992 - val_accuracy: 0.8713
Epoch 7/10
43/43 [==============================] - 1s 31ms/step - loss: 0.2814 - accuracy: 0.8863 - val_loss: 0.3035 - val_accuracy: 0.8713
Epoch 8/10
43/43 [==============================] - 1s 31ms/step - loss: 0.2873 - accuracy: 0.8863 - val_loss: 0.3012 - val_accuracy: 0.8780
Epoch 9/10
43/43 [==============================] - 1s 31ms/step - loss: 0.2809 - accuracy: 0.8869 - val_loss: 0.3078 - val_accuracy: 0.8700
Epoch 10/10
43/43 [==============================] - 1s 31ms/step - loss: 0.2919 - accuracy: 0.8833 - val_loss: 0.2932 - val_accuracy: 0.8747
<keras.callbacks.History at 0x7fc56c264c50>
```

We just have to evaluate our model. "Evaluate" allows a model to be evaluated as its name suggests to get the error rate, just take 100% - the success rate (scores [1]):

```
scores = model.evaluate(X_test, y_test, verbose=0)
print("Model score : %.2f%%" % (scores[1]*100))
print("Model error rate : %.2f%%" % (100-scores[1]*100))
```

You should get:

Model score: 87.47%
Model error rate: 12.53%

b) Medium CNN

Now all we have to do is keeping the same code and only changing the CNN architecture. Note that, all cells from model=sequential() must be executed again.

Our goal is to have:

- A convolution of 32 filters in 5 × 5 kernel with a ReLU (don't forget the input_shape parameter).

- A 2 × 2 max-pooling.

- A dropout of 0.2.

- A flatten layer.

- A dense of 128 units with a ReLU.

- A dense of 2 units with a softmax.

Compared to small CNN, you need to add the max-pooling and dropout to encode everything. The max-pooling is added thanks to MaxPooling2D, which takes as a parameter the dimensions of the pooling (2,2) in the parameter pool_size. The dropout for its part is added via Dropout, which directly receives the dropout rate (i.e. 0.2). This means that 20% of neurons will be ignored:

```python
model.add(Conv2D(32, (5, 5), input_shape=(3, 50, 50), activation='relu'))
model.add(MaxPooling2D(pool_size=(2, 2)))
model.add(Dropout(0.2))
model.add(Flatten())
model.add(Dense(128, activation='relu'))
model.add(Dense(num_classes, activation='softmax'))
```

The rest of the code being the same, you can start training the network and get the following result:

```
Epoch 1/10
43/43 [==============================] - 3s 32ms/step - loss: 1.1115 - accuracy: 0.6973 - val_loss: 0.5761 - val_accuracy: 0.7360
Epoch 2/10
43/43 [==============================] - 1s 20ms/step - loss: 0.5714 - accuracy: 0.7289 - val_loss: 0.5625 - val_accuracy: 0.7360
Epoch 3/10
43/43 [==============================] - 1s 20ms/step - loss: 0.5528 - accuracy: 0.7419 - val_loss: 0.5616 - val_accuracy: 0.7360
Epoch 4/10
43/43 [==============================] - 1s 22ms/step - loss: 0.5602 - accuracy: 0.7341 - val_loss: 0.5602 - val_accuracy: 0.7360
Epoch 5/10
43/43 [==============================] - 1s 20ms/step - loss: 0.5611 - accuracy: 0.7312 - val_loss: 0.5586 - val_accuracy: 0.7360
Epoch 6/10
43/43 [==============================] - 1s 20ms/step - loss: 0.5683 - accuracy: 0.7232 - val_loss: 0.5577 - val_accuracy: 0.7360
Epoch 7/10
43/43 [==============================] - 1s 20ms/step - loss: 0.5579 - accuracy: 0.7331 - val_loss: 0.5561 - val_accuracy: 0.7360
Epoch 8/10
43/43 [==============================] - 1s 20ms/step - loss: 0.5512 - accuracy: 0.7364 - val_loss: 0.5540 - val_accuracy: 0.7360
Epoch 9/10
43/43 [==============================] - 1s 20ms/step - loss: 0.5502 - accuracy: 0.7319 - val_loss: 0.5357 - val_accuracy: 0.7360
Epoch 10/10
43/43 [==============================] - 1s 20ms/step - loss: 0.5410 - accuracy: 0.7215 - val_loss: 0.5135 - val_accuracy: 0.7360
<keras.callbacks.History at 0x7f8c62acf650>
```

And by evaluating the model, you get:

Model score : 73.60%
Model error rate : 26.40%

c) Large CNN

For large CNN, we will duplicate the medium CNN. Here is the target architecture:

- A convolution of 30 filters in 5 × 5 kernel with a ReLU activation (don't forget the input_shape)

- A 2 × 2 max-pooling

- A convolution of 15 filters in 3 × 3 kernel with ReLU

- A dropout of 0.2

- A flatten layer

- A dense of 128 units with ReLU

- A dense 50 of units with ReLU

- A dense 10 of units with softmax

Here is the full code of the method:

```python
model.add(Conv2D(30, (5, 5), input_shape=(3, 50, 50), activation='relu'))
model.add(MaxPooling2D(pool_size=(2, 2)))
model.add(Conv2D(15, (3, 3), activation='relu'))
model.add(MaxPooling2D(pool_size=(2, 2)))
model.add(Dropout(0.2))
model.add(Flatten())
model.add(Dense(128, activation='relu'))
model.add(Dense(50, activation='relu'))
model.add(Dense(num_classes, activation='softmax'))
```

After training, you should obtain:

```
Epoch 1/10
43/43 [==============================] - 45s 32ms/step - loss: 0.6746 - accuracy: 0.5897 - val_loss: 0.6406 - val_accuracy: 0.6000
Epoch 2/10
43/43 [==============================] - 1s 15ms/step - loss: 0.6337 - accuracy: 0.6135 - val_loss: 0.5903 - val_accuracy: 0.6947
Epoch 3/10
43/43 [==============================] - 1s 15ms/step - loss: 0.5971 - accuracy: 0.6815 - val_loss: 0.5844 - val_accuracy: 0.6860
Epoch 4/10
43/43 [==============================] - 1s 15ms/step - loss: 0.5789 - accuracy: 0.7041 - val_loss: 0.5467 - val_accuracy: 0.7327
Epoch 5/10
43/43 [==============================] - 1s 15ms/step - loss: 0.5324 - accuracy: 0.7453 - val_loss: 0.4763 - val_accuracy: 0.7880
Epoch 6/10
43/43 [==============================] - 1s 15ms/step - loss: 0.5083 - accuracy: 0.7678 - val_loss: 0.4512 - val_accuracy: 0.8120
Epoch 7/10
43/43 [==============================] - 1s 15ms/step - loss: 0.4948 - accuracy: 0.7836 - val_loss: 0.4493 - val_accuracy: 0.8073
Epoch 8/10
43/43 [==============================] - 1s 15ms/step - loss: 0.4761 - accuracy: 0.7940 - val_loss: 0.4758 - val_accuracy: 0.7973
Epoch 9/10
43/43 [==============================] - 1s 15ms/step - loss: 0.4618 - accuracy: 0.8085 - val_loss: 0.4254 - val_accuracy: 0.8247
Epoch 10/10
43/43 [==============================] - 1s 15ms/step - loss: 0.4556 - accuracy: 0.8061 - val_loss: 0.4489 - val_accuracy: 0.8013
<keras.callbacks.History at 0x7f27703321d0>
```

And by evaluating the model, you get:

Model score: 80.13%
Model error rate: 19.87%

4. Exploit a pre-trained model with different fine-tuning methods

First of all, I encourage you to remember the possible strategies introduced in the previous section: total fine-tuning, feature extraction, and partial fine-tuning. In the three cases, it is necessary to replace the last fully-connected layers which make it possible to classify the image in one of the 1000 ImageNet classes) by a classifier more suited to our problem. For example, since we want to differentiate malignant from benign (binary classification). Removing the last layer is done by adding the include_top = False argument when importing the pre-trained model. In this case, you must also specify the dimensions of the input images (input_shape):

```python
from keras.applications.vgg16 import VGG16
from keras.layers import Dense, Flatten
from keras import Model
vggmodel = VGG16(weights="imagenet", include_top=False,input_shape=(3, 50, 50))
vggmodel.summary()
```

Use a Sequential model to add a trainable classifier on top:

```
from keras.models import Sequential
from keras.layers.core import Dense,Flatten
model = Sequential()

for layer in vggmodel.layers:
    model.add(layer)

model.add(Flatten())
model.add(Dense(2, activation='softmax'))
model.summary()
```

Note that, it is recommended to use sigmoid for binary classification but softmax works also just fine. If you want to replace softmax with sigmoid, you have to also consider changing 'categorical_crossentropy' in model.compile to 'binary_crossentropy'.

a) Use the entire architecture of the model

After training, you should obtain:

```
Epoch 1/10
43/43 [==============================] - 11s 218ms/step - loss: 2.9301 - accuracy: 0.5897 - val_loss: 0.6869 - val_accuracy: 0.6140
Epoch 2/10
43/43 [==============================] - 9s 205ms/step - loss: 0.6717 - accuracy: 0.5988 - val_loss: 0.5863 - val_accuracy: 0.6640
Epoch 3/10
43/43 [==============================] - 9s 205ms/step - loss: 0.5673 - accuracy: 0.7183 - val_loss: 0.5082 - val_accuracy: 0.7653
Epoch 4/10
43/43 [==============================] - 9s 206ms/step - loss: 0.5306 - accuracy: 0.7470 - val_loss: 0.5317 - val_accuracy: 0.7520
Epoch 5/10
43/43 [==============================] - 9s 207ms/step - loss: 0.5131 - accuracy: 0.7586 - val_loss: 0.5055 - val_accuracy: 0.7733
Epoch 6/10
43/43 [==============================] - 9s 206ms/step - loss: 0.4996 - accuracy: 0.7639 - val_loss: 0.4790 - val_accuracy: 0.7880
Epoch 7/10
43/43 [==============================] - 9s 207ms/step - loss: 0.5039 - accuracy: 0.7576 - val_loss: 0.5056 - val_accuracy: 0.7633
Epoch 8/10
43/43 [==============================] - 9s 208ms/step - loss: 0.4985 - accuracy: 0.7640 - val_loss: 0.5070 - val_accuracy: 0.7760
Epoch 9/10
43/43 [==============================] - 9s 208ms/step - loss: 0.4759 - accuracy: 0.7856 - val_loss: 0.4543 - val_accuracy: 0.7953
Epoch 10/10
43/43 [==============================] - 9s 208ms/step - loss: 0.4903 - accuracy: 0.7700 - val_loss: 0.4544 - val_accuracy: 0.7860
<keras.callbacks.History at 0x7efc80a930d0>
```

And by evaluating the model, you get:

Model score: 78.60%
Model error rate: 21.40%

b) Train some layers while freeze others

We train the new classifier and the upper layers:

```
# Do not train the first 4 layers (lowest)
# This code must be added before sequential
for layer in vggmodel.layers[:5]:
    layer.trainable = False
```

After training, you should obtain:

```
Epoch 1/10
43/43 [==============================] - 9s 168ms/step - loss: 0.6697 - accuracy: 0.6091 - val_loss: 0.6675 - val_accuracy: 0.6140
Epoch 2/10
43/43 [==============================] - 7s 154ms/step - loss: 0.6691 - accuracy: 0.6099 - val_loss: 0.6673 - val_accuracy: 0.6140
Epoch 3/10
43/43 [==============================] - 7s 154ms/step - loss: 0.6761 - accuracy: 0.5925 - val_loss: 0.6673 - val_accuracy: 0.6140
Epoch 4/10
43/43 [==============================] - 7s 155ms/step - loss: 0.6743 - accuracy: 0.5970 - val_loss: 0.6671 - val_accuracy: 0.6140
Epoch 5/10
43/43 [==============================] - 7s 155ms/step - loss: 0.6730 - accuracy: 0.6001 - val_loss: 0.6671 - val_accuracy: 0.6140
Epoch 6/10
43/43 [==============================] - 7s 155ms/step - loss: 0.6723 - accuracy: 0.6017 - val_loss: 0.6672 - val_accuracy: 0.6140
Epoch 7/10
43/43 [==============================] - 7s 155ms/step - loss: 0.6716 - accuracy: 0.6034 - val_loss: 0.6671 - val_accuracy: 0.6140
Epoch 8/10
43/43 [==============================] - 7s 155ms/step - loss: 0.6688 - accuracy: 0.6101 - val_loss: 0.6671 - val_accuracy: 0.6140
Epoch 9/10
43/43 [==============================] - 7s 154ms/step - loss: 0.6732 - accuracy: 0.5997 - val_loss: 0.6672 - val_accuracy: 0.6140
Epoch 10/10
43/43 [==============================] - 7s 154ms/step - loss: 0.6730 - accuracy: 0.6000 - val_loss: 0.6671 - val_accuracy: 0.6140
<keras.callbacks.History at 0x7efc7675e350>
```

And by evaluating the model, you get:

> Model score: 61.40%
> Model error rate: 38.60%

c) Feature extraction

We only train the new classifier and we do not re-train the other layers:

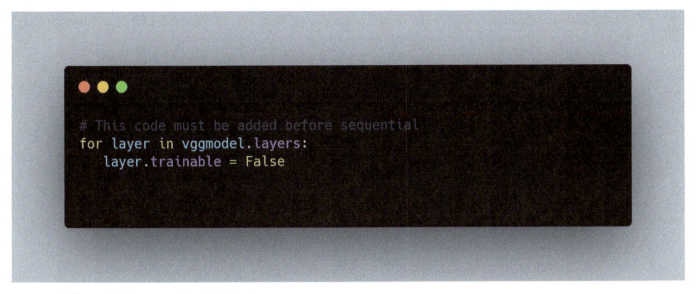

```
# This code must be added before sequential
for layer in vggmodel.layers:
    layer.trainable = False
```

After training, you should obtain:

```
Epoch 1/10
43/43 [==============================] - 5s 87ms/step - loss: 0.7200 - accuracy: 0.5040 - val_loss: 0.6516 - val_accuracy: 0.6353
Epoch 2/10
43/43 [==============================] - 3s 73ms/step - loss: 0.6452 - accuracy: 0.6402 - val_loss: 0.6202 - val_accuracy: 0.6800
Epoch 3/10
43/43 [==============================] - 3s 73ms/step - loss: 0.6139 - accuracy: 0.6871 - val_loss: 0.6028 - val_accuracy: 0.7013
Epoch 4/10
43/43 [==============================] - 3s 73ms/step - loss: 0.6000 - accuracy: 0.6925 - val_loss: 0.5921 - val_accuracy: 0.7020
Epoch 5/10
43/43 [==============================] - 3s 73ms/step - loss: 0.5787 - accuracy: 0.7125 - val_loss: 0.5841 - val_accuracy: 0.7073
Epoch 6/10
43/43 [==============================] - 3s 74ms/step - loss: 0.5865 - accuracy: 0.6964 - val_loss: 0.5786 - val_accuracy: 0.7140
Epoch 7/10
43/43 [==============================] - 3s 74ms/step - loss: 0.5725 - accuracy: 0.7113 - val_loss: 0.5740 - val_accuracy: 0.7133
Epoch 8/10
43/43 [==============================] - 3s 74ms/step - loss: 0.5774 - accuracy: 0.7036 - val_loss: 0.5700 - val_accuracy: 0.7193
Epoch 9/10
43/43 [==============================] - 3s 74ms/step - loss: 0.5676 - accuracy: 0.7132 - val_loss: 0.5701 - val_accuracy: 0.7253
Epoch 10/10
43/43 [==============================] - 3s 76ms/step - loss: 0.5737 - accuracy: 0.7096 - val_loss: 0.5635 - val_accuracy: 0.7233
<keras.callbacks.History at 0x7efc7898cb90>
```

And by evaluating the model, you get:

Model score: 72.33%
Model error rate: 27.67%

5. Learning curves

Learning curves are frequently used in machine learning for algorithms that optimize their internal parameters gradually over time, such as deep learning neural networks.

- **Train Learning Curve**: The learning curve is a measurement of how well the model is learning based on the training data.

- **Validation Learning Curve**: The learning curve is derived from a hold-out validation dataset and shows how effectively the model generalizes.

Let's plot the curve of VGG16 (feature extractor). First add in the model.fit a variable 'history' as follows:

```
history=model.fit(X_train, y_train, validation_data=(X_test, y_test), epochs=10, batch_size=200)
```

To plot the learning curve for loss, you have to add this portion of code:

```python
import matplotlib.pyplot as plt
print("\n")
print(history.history.keys())
plt.plot(history.history['loss'])
plt.plot(history.history['val_loss'])
plt.title('model loss')
plt.ylabel('loss')
plt.xlabel('epoch')
plt.legend(['train', 'test'], loc='upper left')
plt.show()
```

We will obtain (Figure 43):

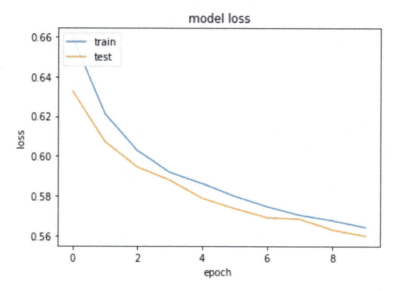

Figure 41: Loss learning curve for VGG16 trained as feature extractor

We can also plot the learning curve for accuracy, by adding this code:

```
plt.plot(history.history['accuracy'])
plt.plot(history.history['val_accuracy'])
plt.title('model accuracy')
plt.ylabel('accuracy')
plt.xlabel('epoch')
plt.legend(['train', 'test'], loc='upper left')
plt.show()
```

We will obtain (Figure 42):

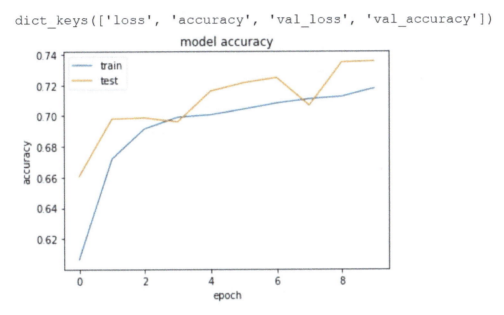

Figure 42: Accuracy learning curve for VGG16 trained as feature extractor

Conclusion

In this chapter, I have presented the development tools, the architectures of the exploited pre-trained models and Datasets. For the implementation part, we built models from scratch and exploited VGG16 with different fine-tuning methods, as we have seen the complete process of building models from data preparation to plotting the learning curves.

General Conclusion

In the theoretical part, we saw in detail CAD and how a convolutional neural network works. In particular, we were able to understand what the different elements of the architecture were doing (convolutions, pooling, proofreading, flattening, dense, etc.) and discovered real networks used in production (ResNet, DenseNet and VGG in particular).

In the practical part, we learned how to process data and set up three convolutional neural networks with different architectures and we compared the results. Additionally, we fine-tuned VGG16 with different transfer learning methods and plot learning curves for it.

Now you will be able to apply the same steps on DDSM and try other pre-trained models for classification.

References

[1] https://www.wikipedia.org , Computer-aided diagnosis, (visualized 19/03/2020).

[2] https://www.unice.fr, Option de traitement d'images Mémento pour la séance N°6, (visualized 02/04/2020).

[3] R. C.Gonzalez, R. E. Wood, Digital Image Processing, 3rd Edition, Published by Prentice Hall, 2008.

[4] A. Krishnan, K. Sreekumar, International Journal of Computer Science and Information Technologies, Vol. 5 (6), 7877-7879, 2014.

[5] J. Brownlee, How to Choose a Feature Selection Method For Machine Learning, published in Python Machine Learning, 2019 (visualized 07/04/2020).

[6] https://www.wikipedia.org , Feature (machine learning), (visualized 18/04/2020).

[7] B. Halalli, A. Makandar, Computer-Aided Diagnosis – Medical Image analysis Techniques, Published in IntechOpen, DOI:10.5772/Intechopen.69792, 2017.

[8] http://www.differencebetween.net , Difference between Clustering and Classification, (visualized 23/04/2020).

[10] S.S. Shai,B.D. Shai, Understanding Machine Learning: From Theory to Algorithms, Published by Cambridge University Press, 2014.

[11] P. Dangeti, Statistics for Machine Learning, Published by Packt Publishing, 2017.

[12] C. Gagnè, Apprentissage et reconnaissance, université LAVAL, 2016.

[13] https://www.verywellmind.com, An Overview of the Different Parts of a Neuron, (visualized 25/04/2020).

[14] G Zaccone, K. Rezaul, A. Menshawy, Deep Learning with TensorFlow, Published by Packt Publishing, 2017.

[15] N. Ketkar, Deep Learning with Python: A Hands-on Introduction, Published by Springer Science+Business Media New York, 2017.

[16] R. Bonnin, Building Machine Learning Projects with TensorFlow, Published by Packt Publishing, 2016.

[17] S. Skansi, Introduction to Deep Learning from Logical Calculus to Artificial Intelligence, Springer International Publishing AG, 2018.

[18] V. Zocca, G.Spacagna, D. Slater, P. Roelants, Python Deep, Published by Packt Publishing, 2017.

[19] https://www.anaconda.com,distribution, , (visualized 28/04/2020).

[20] https://jupyter-notebook.readthedocs.io, The Jupyter Notebook, (visualized 28/04/2020).

[21] https://keras.io, (visualized 28/04/2020).

[22] http://academictorrents.com, Invasive Ductal Carcinoma (IDC) Histology Image Dataset, (visualized 29/04/2020).

[23] https://iq.opengenus.org, VGG16 architecture, (visualized 29/04/2020).

[24] https://towardsdatascience.com , Review: DenseNet - Dense Convolutional Network (Image Classification) , (visualized 30/04/2020).

[25] University of South Florida, http://marathon.csee.usf.edu/ Mammography/Database.html, (visualized 30/04/2020).